SUPER COOL CHEMICAL REACTION ACTIVITIES

with MAX AXIOM

by Agnieszka Biskup

Consultant:
Bridget Alligood DePrince, Ph.D.

... an imprint of Capstone Global Library Limited, a company incorporated in England and Wales having its registered office at 7 Pilgrim Street, London, EC4V 5LB – Registered company number: 6695582

www.raintree.co.uk
myorders@raintree.co.uk

Editorial Credits
Christopher L. Harbo, editor; Nathan Gassman, art director; Tracy McCabe, designer; Katy Lavigne, production specialist; Sarah Schuette and Marcy Morin, project creation

Cover Illustration
Marcelo Baez

Photo Credits
Photographs by Capstone Studio: Karon Dubke

ISBN 978 1 4062 9322 7 (hardback)
18 17 16 15 14
10 9 8 7 6 5 4 3 2 1

ISBN 978 1 4062 9327 2 (paperback)
19 18 17 16
10 9 8 7 6 5 4 3 2 1

British Library Cataloguing in Publication Data
A full catalogue record for this book is available from the British Library.

Printed in China

Contents

Chemical reactions are all around us. Some reactions we can't control, such as the flash of a firefly.

But others we *can* actually control, such as burning wood or setting off fireworks.

In a chemical reaction, one substance changes into a new substance.

This fire changes wood into ash and smoke. It may seem like magic, but it's real!

BUBBLING BLOBS

Oil and water don't mix, and this project uses that fact to its advantage. Check out how a chemical reaction can create a super cool lava lamp.

YOU'LL NEED

clear, clean plastic 500-mL drinks bottle

vegetable oil

water

food colouring

effervescent tablets

PLAN OF ACTION

1. Fill the bottle three-quarters full of vegetable oil. Then slowly pour water into the bottle until it's almost full.

2. Wait a few minutes for the oil and water to separate completely.

3. Add about 12 drops of food colouring.

4. Wait for the food colouring to fall through the oil and mix with the water on the bottom.

5. Break an effervescent tablet into three or four pieces, and drop them into the bottle.

6. Watch the blobs begin to rise!

⚡ AXIOM EXPLANATION

The effervescent tablet reacts with the coloured water to form bubbles of carbon dioxide gas. The gas rises and takes some of the coloured water with it. The gas escapes when it reaches the top of the bottle. The coloured water droplets then fall back down into the bottle.

effervescent bubbling, hissing or foaming as gas escapes

carbon dioxide colourless, odourless gas

ENDOTHERMIC BAGGIES

Some chemical reactions absorb energy and decrease the temperature of their surrounding environment. Try this experiment to feel the effects of an **endothermic reaction** as it happens in the palm of your hand.

YOU'LL NEED

5 mL citric acid*

5 mL bicarbonate soda

1-litre resealable plastic food bag

water

*found at health food shops

PLAN OF ACTION

1. Pour the citric acid and bicarbonate soda into the plastic bag.

Bicarbonate Soda

Citric Acid

2. Shake the bag gently to mix the two ingredients.

3. Pour a small amount of water into the bag and seal it quickly.

4. Hold the bag in the palm of your hand as the chemical reaction takes place.

AXIOM EXPLANATION

Citric acid, bicarbonate soda and water react to produce carbon dioxide. The gas fills and inflates the bag. Because the reaction is endothermic, the liquid in the bag becomes cold to the touch. Once the reaction ends, the mixture returns to room temperature.

endothermic reaction chemical reaction that absorbs energy from its surroundings

acid substance that will react with a base to form a salt; strong acids can burn a person's skin

MONSTER TOOTHPASTE

When it comes to chemical reactions, the most exciting ones are often **exothermic reactions**. They can produce energy as heat – sometimes in surprising ways. Monster toothpaste is one exothermic reaction that never fails to excite a crowd.

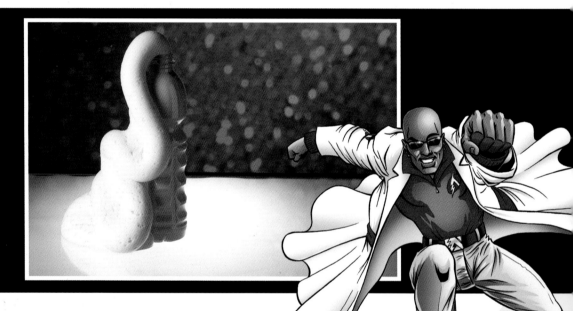

YOU'LL NEED

small bowl

packet of dry yeast

45 mL warm water

clear plastic drinks bottle

foil roasting dish

118 mL of 6% hydrogen peroxide*

washing-up liquid

food colouring

funnel

*found in beauty supply outlets or hair salons

SAFETY FIRST

Put on gloves and safety goggles before attempting this experiment. Hydrogen peroxide can irritate eyes and exposed skin. Wash your hands thoroughly after completing this experiment.

PLAN OF ACTION

1. Mix the yeast and warm water in a small bowl.

2. Set the mixture aside for about 30 seconds, or until the liquid becomes frothy.

3. Place the plastic bottle upright in the middle of the roasting dish. Ask an adult to pour the hydrogen peroxide into the bottle.

4. Put two or three squirts of washing-up liquid into the bottle.

5. Add about 5 drops of food colouring to the bottle.

6. Gently swirl the bottle to mix the ingredients and return it to the middle of the dish.

7. Using the funnel, pour the yeast solution from step 1 into the bottle.

8. Quickly remove the funnel, stand back, and watch the monster toothpaste ooze out!

⚡ AXIOM EXPLANATION

The yeast speeds up the chemical reaction that breaks hydrogen peroxide into oxygen gas and water. The washing-up liquid traps the oxygen, resulting in the formation of foam bubbles. The foam is basically soap and water, so it's safe to touch. Because this is an exothermic reaction, the bottle and foam should feel warm.

exothermic reaction chemical reaction that releases energy to its surroundings

MINI MAGIC FIRE EXTINGUISHER

A fire will keep burning as long as it has fuel, oxygen and heat. This chemical reaction removes one of those ingredients to put out a fire.

YOU'LL NEED

3 votive candles

matches

2-litre clear glass jug

30 mL bicarbonate soda

225 mL vinegar

SAFETY FIRST

Ask an adult for help using candles and matches before attempting this activity.

PLAN OF ACTION

1. Place the candles in a row on a flat surface in an open area outside. Ask an adult to use the matches to light the candles.

2. Place the bicarbonate soda into the jug.

3. Pour in the vinegar. Swirl the liquid in the jug so that the ingredients are well mixed. The mixture will fizz and foam.

4. Slowly tip the jug near the candles without spilling any liquid. Watch what happens to the candle flames.

AXIOM EXPLANATION

When vinegar and bicarbonate soda mix, the chemical reaction forms carbon dioxide gas. Carbon dioxide is heavier than air, so it will stay in the jug longer while it's upright. When the jug is tipped over the flames, the carbon dioxide pours out. It sinks down over the candles, pushing the oxygen out of the way. The flames go out because a fire cannot burn without oxygen.

EGG-CELLENT EGGSPERIMENT

What does an egg look like without a shell? Find out with a chemical reaction which has the power to make an eggshell disappear.

YOU'LL NEED

1 uncooked egg

clear glass jar with lid

vinegar

torch

PLAN OF ACTION

1. Gently place the egg in the jar.

2. Add enough vinegar to completely cover the egg. Screw the lid onto the jar.

3. Let the egg sit in the vinegar for 24 hours at room temperature.

4. Use the lid of the jar to gently strain the vinegar into a sink. Be careful not to let the egg fall out of the jar.

5. Cover the egg with fresh vinegar, and let it sit undisturbed for another two days.

6. Carefully remove the egg from the vinegar. Gently rinse it with water.

7. Shine a torch through the rubbery egg to see the yolk.

⚡ AXIOM EXPLANATION

You may have noticed tiny bubbles all over the egg in the vinegar. These bubbles were carbon dioxide gas. They were produced by a chemical reaction between the vinegar and the eggshell. Vinegar, which contains acetic acid, reacted with the eggshell to dissolve it.

FUNNY BONES

Bones are hard and are likely to break if you try to bend them. This chemical reaction will give you bones that behave in funny ways.

YOU'LL NEED

1 or 2 chicken bones

clear glass jar with lid

vinegar

PLAN OF ACTION

1. Rinse and clean the bones with warm water to make sure all the meat has been removed.

2. Let the bones dry. Note that the bones are hard and do not bend.

3. Place the bones in a jar.

4. Add vinegar to the jar to completely cover the bones. Place the lid on the jar.

5. Let the bones sit for at least 3 days.

6. Remove the bones from the vinegar.

7. Try to bend the bones now. Do they feel any different?

⚡ AXIOM EXPLANATION

Bones contain calcium and phosphorus. These minerals make bones strong and hard. The acetic acid in the vinegar reacts with the minerals. It leaves the remaining materials in the bone soft and rubbery.

calcium soft, silver-white mineral found in teeth and bones

phosphorus mineral in the body found mainly in teeth and bones

POLISHED PENNIES AND COPPER NAILS

Have you ever noticed that pennies turn darker with age? It's all because of chemical reactions. In this two-part experiment, you'll make some old pennies look new again while turning others a little bit green! You'll also make a steel nail look like copper.

YOU'LL NEED

glass or plastic bowl (not metal)

60 mL vinegar

5 mL salt

plastic spoon

20 old, dirty copper pennies*

paper towels

marker pen

kitchen timer

2 clean steel nails

*For best results, use pennies minted before 1992 – they contain more copper than pennies today.

PLAN OF ACTION PART ONE

1. Pour the vinegar into the bowl.

2. Add the salt to the vinegar, and stir it with a plastic spoon until the salt dissolves.

3. Put all the pennies in the bowl.

4. Wait about 5 minutes, then take all the pennies out of the bowl. They should look shiny. Set the bowl of vinegar aside for part two of this experiment.

5. Place 10 of the pennies onto a paper towel to dry.

6. Rinse the other 10 pennies under running water, and put them onto another paper towel to dry. Write "rinsed" on that paper towel with a marker pen so you know which is which.

Rinsed

7. Set the kitchen timer for 1 hour and leave your rinsed pennies to dry. In the meantime, proceed to part two of this experiment.

continued

1. Submerge one steel nail into the leftover salt/vinegar liquid.

2. Place the other steel nail half-in and half-out of the liquid by leaning it against the side of the bowl.

3. Let the nails sit for the remainder of the time left on the kitchen timer you set in part one.

4. When the timer goes off, go and see how your pennies and nails look.

⚡ AXIOM EXPLANATION

New pennies turn a dirty brown over time because copper reacts with oxygen in the air. A dark substance called copper oxide forms on the surface. The acetic acid in the vinegar removes the copper oxide from the pennies, making them bright and shiny again.

Rinsing the pennies under water stops the chemical reaction. The salt/vinegar mix left on the unrinsed pennies allows the chemical reaction to continue, forming a blue-green chemical coating.

The vinegar/salt solution removed some of the copper from the pennies, which remains in the liquid. When the steel nails are placed in the liquid, the copper is attracted to the metal of the nail. The result is copper-coated nails!

LACTIC PLASTIC

In the early 1900s, **casein** plastic was used to make jewellery, buttons, combs and buckles. Surprisingly, this plastic was made using ordinary cow's milk. With a simple chemical reaction, you can make your very own casein plastic.

YOU'LL NEED

225 mL whole milk

small saucepan

small bowl

20 mL vinegar

food colouring

spoon

fine mesh strainer

large bowl

paper towels

casein type of protein found in milk

continued

PLAN OF ACTION

1. Ask an adult to heat the milk in a saucepan on the hob. Heat until the milk is very hot but not boiling.

2. Ask an adult to pour the hot milk into a small bowl.

3. Add the vinegar and 5 drops of food colouring to the milk.

4. Stir the mixture slowly with a spoon for about a minute.

5. Carefully pour the milk through the strainer into a larger bowl. Some clumps should remain in the strainer. Pour any liquid left in the bowl down the drain.

6. Let the clumps cool for a few minutes. Put them onto a paper towel, and press them gently with another paper towel to soak up any extra moisture.

7. Knead the clumps together with your fingers to make a ball. You have just made a ball of casein plastic.

8. Mould your plastic into a shape.

9. Put your moulded plastic on a plate to dry and harden for two days.

⚡ **AXIOM EXPLANATION**

Milk is full of a *protein* called casein. The combination of heat and acetic acid from the vinegar makes the milk curdle. This process pulls the casein proteins out of the milk to form rubbery clumps called curds. The casein curds make up the plastic you can form into various shapes.

protein chemical made by animal and plant cells to carry out various functions

GLUE GOO

Sometimes chemistry can be a bit gooey. Create a home-made version of slime using the power of cross-linking **molecules**!

YOU'LL NEED

2 plastic disposable cups

5 mL Borax powder*

118 mL water

plastic spoon

118 mL white craft glue

food colouring

glass bowl

*found at the supermarket on the washing powder/laundry aisle

PLAN OF ACTION

1. Add the Borax powder and half of the water to a plastic cup. Stir well with the plastic spoon, then set aside.

2. Pour the glue into a second plastic cup.

3. Add the remaining water and a few drops of food colouring to the cup with the glue in it.

4. Use the plastic spoon to stir the glue-water mixture well.

5. Pour the contents of both cups into the bowl. Stir well. The slime will form before your very eyes.

6. Let it sit for about 30 seconds before you pull it out to play with. Put the slime in a sealed plastic bag to stop it drying out.

⚡ AXIOM EXPLANATION

White craft glue is a polymer. It is made up of long chains of molecules of a substance called polyvinyl acetate. The chains easily slip and slide against each other, allowing the glue to be poured. When you add the Borax and water solution to the glue, a chemical reaction occurs. The long glue molecule chains get cross-linked together to form the rubbery, stretchy, gooey stuff we call slime.

molecule group of two or more atoms bonded together; a molecule is the smallest part of a substance that cannot be divided without a chemical change

polymer natural or synthetic compound made up of small, simple molecules linked together in long chains of repeating units

MAGIC COLOUR CHANGE

Sometimes a chemical reaction can look like magic. This show-stopping experiment makes an astounding colour change that happens in the blink of an eye!

YOU'LL NEED

2 500-milligram vitamin C tablets*

plastic sandwich bag

metal spoon

measuring spoons

3 disposable clear plastic cups, labelled "1," "2" and "3"

warm water

plastic spoons for stirring

5 mL of 2% tincture of iod

15 mL of 3% hydrogen pero

2 mL liquid laundry starch

stopwatch

*find these items in a pharmacy

SAFETY FIRST

Remember to wear safety goggles and gloves while handling iodine and hydrogen peroxide in this experiment.

PLAN OF ACTION

1. Put the vitamin C tablets into the plastic bag. Crush them into a fine powder using the back of a metal spoon.

2. Pour the crushed powder into Cup 1. Then add 60 mL of warm water to the cup.

3. Stir for at least 30 seconds with a plastic spoon. The liquid may be cloudy.

4. Scoop 5 mL of the liquid out of Cup 1 and place it into Cup 2.

continued

5. Add 60 mL of warm water and the iodine to Cup 2. Has the brown iodine become clear?

6. Add 60 mL of warm water, the hydrogen peroxide and the liquid laundry starch to Cup 3.

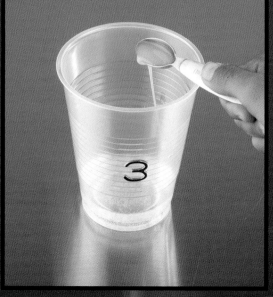

7. Pour all of the liquid from Cup 2 into Cup 3 and start your stopwatch. Now pour the liquid back and forth between Cup 3 and Cup 2 a couple of times.

8. Put the cup down onto a table and watch the liquid. The colourless liquid will turn dark blue in a flash! Check your stopwatch to see how long the reaction took.

9. Now add 30 mL of liquid from Cup 1 into the cup with blue liquid. Stir well. Your dark blue liquid will suddenly become clear again!

⚡ AXIOM EXPLANATION

This experiment may seem like magic – but it's science. It is called an iodine clock reaction. Scientists use clock reactions to study the rates of chemical reactions. They can determine how fast *reactants* are used up or *products* appear.

When iodine and starch make contact, they react to form a new dark blue substance. But the vitamin C prevents the iodine from reacting with the starch. The colour change will only occur after all the vitamin C has been used up. This experiment is a chemical battle between the starch and the vitamin C. The starch wants to make the iodine blue. The vitamin C is trying to stop the blue reaction from happening at all!

reactant substance that undergoes a chemical change in a chemical reaction

product substances that are produced from a chemical reaction

Glossary

acid substance that will react with a base to form a salt; strong acids can burn a person's skin

calcium soft, silver-white mineral found in teeth and bones

carbon dioxide colourless, odourless gas

casein type of protein found in milk

effervescent bubbling, hissing or foaming as gas escapes

endothermic reaction chemical reaction that absorbs energy from its surroundings

exothermic reaction chemical reaction that releases energy to its surroundings

molecule group of two or more atoms bonded together; a molecule is the smallest part of a substance that cannot be divided without a chemical change

phosphorus mineral in the body found mainly in teeth and bones

polymer natural or synthetic compound made up of small, simple molecules linked together in long chains of repeating units

product substances that are produced from a chemical reaction

protein chemical made by animal and plant cells to carry out various functions

reactant substance that undergoes a chemical change in a chemical reaction

Read More

Chemical Reactions: Investigating an Industrial Accident, (Anatomy of an Investigation), Richard Spilsbury (Raintree, 2014)

It's Elementary! Putting the crackle into chemistry, Robert Winston (Dorling Kindersley, 2010)

Solids, Liquids and Gases (Essential Physical Science), Louise Spilsbury and Richard Spilsbury (Raintree, 2013)

Websites

www.bbc.co.uk/education/guides/zqd2mp3/video
Join Dr Peter Wothers and his Alchemist's Apprentices as he conducts chemistry experiments in his laboratory.

www.sciencecentres.org.uk
Explore the UK Association for Science and Discovery Centres' website and find out how to get involved in exciting science workshops near you.

www.sciencemuseum.org.uk
Explore the Science Museum's games page and play the Team Plastics game - create an awesome team capable of developing a new plastic.

Index